ART FROM THE
CARMEL MISSION

GAIL SHERIDAN

MARY PAT MCCORMICK

PHOTOGRAPHY BY DENNIS WYSZYNSKI

MISSION SAN CARLOS BORROMÉO DEL RÍO CARMELO

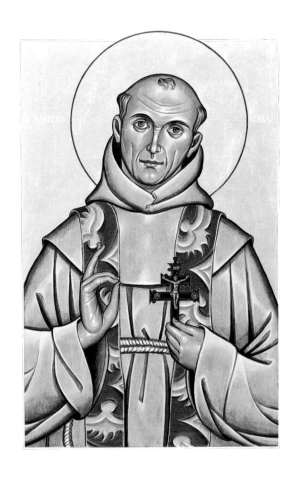

DEDICATED TO FATHER JUNÍPERO SERRA

FOUNDER AND PRESIDENTE

OF THE ALTA CALIFORNIA MISSIONS

IN HONOR OF THE

300TH ANNIVERSARY OF HIS BIRTH

1713–1784

ART FROM THE CARMEL MISSION

© Carmel Mission

Published in 2011 by the Carmel Mission, Carmel, California in cooperation with Fine Arts Press (www.fineartspress.com).

ISBN 978 0 615 44335-5 (hard cover)
ISBN 978 0 615 44728-5 (soft cover)

Publication design and composition by Ron Shore, Shore Design

Photography by Dennis Wyszynski

Editing by Sandra Berris

cover: *The Fourteenth Station of the Cross* (see page 48 for details)
José María Uriarte, Mexico, circa 1802, oil on canvas
a set of 14 paintings, 42" x 34" each

back cover: *Zacatecas Sketch of Father Serra*
Anonymous, Mexico, 19th century, tempera on paper, 12" x 9$^1/_2$"

Harry Downie, chief restorer at the Mission from 1930 to 1980, undertook many research travels regarding Father Serra and mission architecture. One such trip was to Mexico by automobile with his family. He was asleep in the back seat of the family car headed toward Zacatecas. Downie claimed that something woke him, before his family did, urging him to rummage through a second-hand store in the town. On entering the back room, he discovered the sketch covered with dust. He knew it was a unique find.

This work may capture a truer image of Father Serra than others. Historical documentation states he posed for a portrait in Mexico. However, the paper of the Mission's sketch is from the 1800s, while the inscription indicates a work of 1776–1777. Therefore, it appears to be a copy of a Mexican portrait.

The translated inscription is:

"Father Junipero Serra Founder of the Holy Mission of San Diego, San Carlos Borromeo of Monterey, San Gabriel, San Luis Obispo, San Francisco of Assisi and San Juan Capistrano of Upper California-Sketch by Pedro Pablo Márquez Convent of the Holy Cross Province of the Holy Gospel in Querétaro"

Carmel Mission Summer Solstice, June 2007, page 22
photograph by Richard Shea, Carmel, CA.

Carmel Mission
3080 Rio Road Carmel, California 93923
831.624.1271
www.carmelmission.org

Printed in Hong Kong

TABLE OF CONTENTS

Virgin of Light (see page 90 for details)

LET US LOOK AGAIN, AND MORE CLOSELY

When I began to systematically visit the California missions over ten years ago, I was both amazed and disconcerted at what I found. Many of the works of painting, sculpture, metal and textile arts from the Spanish Colonial period that I saw at the missions are truly extraordinary. What was disconcerting, however, was the fact that few people seemed to know much about them, and that most of these objects have not been seriously studied and published. The same realization occurred again and again at other missions in Northern Mexico and Southwest United States. This was one of the principal motives that led Michael Komenecky and me to organize an international exhibition about the arts of the missions of northern New Spain in 2009. The lack of knowledge and few publications do not mean, of course, that no one cares, but it is a situation that exposes art works to the dangers of theft or damage, which would deprive us, and those who come after us, of the insights into human capacities and diversity that these objects embody. The importance of this catalogue is that it is a significant preventive step in the efforts to conserve and understand cultural heritage.

Over the years, I have met many people in California who are aware of the importance of the art works of the missions for the history of their communities, at least, and in some instances, much beyond. For instance, I was fortunate to have known Norman Neuerburg, who, shortly before his death in 1987, was invited by the National University in Mexico City to tell us about these buildings and especially about the objects that they contain, most of which originally came from central New Spain (Mexico). It was then that I learned of a unique painting that can serve as an example of some of the reasons why mission art works are worth saving.

Norman was studying a painting of the Virgen de la Luz now at the San Diego Presidio. Instead of the white male soul that is usually represented in this composition, the Virgin Mary at San Diego is saving an Indian soul, while other natives, St. Francis of Assisi and St. Joseph look on. We drove together to León, Guanajuato, where the oldest painting of the Virgen de la Luz in the American continent is to be found. The small canvas, brought from Sicily to New Spain by a Jesuit missionary in the early eighteenth century, is still the main focus of veneration in the cathedral of León, which was formerly the Jesuit church. Like other Jesuit ideas, as well as objects, the Virgen de la Luz was adopted by the Franciscans and introduced to the last missions they established among native Americans: those in California. The San Diego painting shows that the Franciscans—perhaps Junípero Serra himself in this case, since he founded the San Diego mission—took a proactive attitude towards imagery. They were open to changing established subject matter to include the indigenous people they meant to convert to Christianity and to Spanish ways.

There exists another painting of the Virgen de la Luz in California, this one with a Franciscan donor at the lower right corner, and it is to be seen at Serra's second mission: San Carlos Borromeo del Río Carmelo. This last painting is one of the works reproduced, for the first time in full, in this book. Judging from the brief history of the representations of the Virgen de la Luz just sketched out, this particular image of the Virgin obviously was important to the Franciscans in California. The publication of a photograph of the Carmel painting, with an explanatory text, will now make it easier to study all of these works in greater depth. There is more to be said about all of these objects, and about all of the works illustrated in this catalogue.

The information published here is a starting point from which to gain better knowledge of what the missionaries thought they were doing, and how they went about it, but also of how native Americans, Spaniards, Mexicans and Americans have seen and used these works over the centuries. The production of this volume, which joins the other precious few publications about the paintings and sculptures still at the California missions, is an important service. It is my hope and expectation that fresh ideas about the Franciscan California mission experience will emerge as a result of this new resource.

CLARA BARGELLINI
Universidad Nacional Autónoma de México

Baptism of Jesus by John the Baptist (see page 68 for details)

The Carmel Mission Docent Association was founded in 2005 as a volunteer organization to share mission history and art through its programs and tours for visitors. For many years, The Docent Association was nurtured and advised by Rosellen and Lou Sanna, former Director of Stewardship and former Director of Facilities and Curator of the Museum, respectively. Their support and inspiration launched the Association.

In 2006, the Association established inventory and art research teams. The purpose of these teams was to research and document the facts known about the art, sculpture, silver and vestments of the Carmel Mission. This catalog is based on the research conducted by the individuals on those teams. Without their work, this catalog would not have been possible. We are grateful for their detailed study and their passion. We especially wish to acknowledge Maureen Bianchini, chair of the art research team, for her dedication to the research and for the leadership she provided in recruiting and supporting the researchers over many years. Research papers, including those written by the authors, were provided by the following individuals and were the basis for the text we have compiled: Maureen Bianchini, Mahlon Coleman, Robin Domiter, Pamela Huckins, Joyce Merritt, Karen Walker, Linda Wilde and Madonna Zelitti. A special thanks to Mary Ann Pirotte who has diligently kept an electronic inventory of the works of art for many years.

We were considerably motivated by Dr. Clara Bargellini, world authority on Spanish Colonial art at the Instituto de Investigaciones Estéticas of the Universidad Nacional Autónoma de México, Mexico City, Mexico. Dr. Bargellini visited the Carmel collection in conjunction with the development of an exhibition and related catalog, *The Arts of the Missions of Northern New Spain 1600–1821*, which opened at the Antiguo Colegio de San Ildefonso in Mexico City in 2009, and then went on to the San Antonio Museum of Art, the Museo Amparo in Puebla, the Centro Cultural Tijuana, and the Oakland Museum of California. Her information, knowledge and enthusiasm for the collection gave us the impetus for pursuing this project. She has graciously contributed the Forward to this catalog.

There were many technical challenges associated with photographing the art, especially in the Basilica. We were very pleased with our photographer, Dennis Wyszynski, who found ways to eclipse these issues and spent weeks obtaining the best images possible for the catalog. Mission staff member, Huu Nguyen, was very helpful in facilitating Dennis' work. The reredos solstice photo was used with the permission of photographer Richard Shea. Our book designer, Ron Shore, gave us much needed direction, creative ideas, a beautiful book layout and demonstrated great patience as we moved the project forward. All of these experienced professionals contributed to a publication we hope visitors will enjoy.

A special thanks goes to Sandy Berris who spent hours editing our writing and encouraged and advised us along the way. Dr. Julianne Burton-Carvajal was instrumental in helping structure the format for early research papers and made recommendations about research sources. Linda Andrews and Alejandro Reyes-Vizzuet, conservators of several mission statues, gave us access to photographs and information about the condition of these pieces. Dr. Alice M. Zrebiec, Consulting Curator, Textile Art, Denver Art Museum provided information and resources about liturgical vestments along with Father Gregory Adolph of the Diocese of Tucson, Arizona.

Gwen Smith and Liz Tanna graciously gave us time and support when it was needed. Father John Griffin, V.C., our pastor, has always shown encouragement for this work and made available his time and talent in supporting the research, pursuing restoration projects funded by the Carmel community and for championing publication of this catalog.

The journey from research to publication has been challenging and rewarding. Our spouses, Ralph Love and Dick McCormick, have provided encouragement, support and love throughout the process. We feel so blessed and are grateful for their presence in our lives.

Finally, none of this would have been possible without the community of Carmel Mission who embraced our work and without the financial support of the following organizations and individuals:

THE CARMEL MISSION DOCENT ASSOCIATION

BASZUCKI FAMILY FOUNDATION

BRIAN A. AND SANDRA E. BERRIS

GARY AND MARY CARY COUGHLAN

JOSEPHINE JEWETT DI GIORGIO

THOMAS AND LORRAINE ELLZEY

RONALD L. JACOBSON

RICHARD AND MARY PAT MCCORMICK

RICHARD AND ELIZABETH MOLEY

W. E. (BILL) REICHMUTH

RALPH LOVE AND GAIL SHERIDAN

BERNICE SHERIDAN

VIVIAN SWEENEY

SAMUEL L. WRIGHT FAMILY TRUST

Gail Sheridan and Mary Pat McCormick, February 2011

The authors are active members of the Carmel Mission Docent Association. They conduct art research and lead tours of the historical mission grounds and its art and artifacts.

Ms. Sheridan holds a B.A. in Political Science and an M.A. in American Studies.
Ms. McCormick holds a B.S. in Elementary Education and an M.A. in Liberal Arts.

Founding Painting (detail, see page 92) Léon Trousset, California, USA, 1877, oil on canvas, 53" x 72"

FATHER SERRA AND THE MISSIONARIES

Father Serra was born in 1713 in Mallorca, Spain. He was born Miguel José Serra and entered the Franciscan seminary at the age of 16 taking the name Junípero in honor of a companion of St. Francis. He entered the Order of Friars Minor (O.F.M.) in 1730. He studied at the Lullian University in the city of Palma, Mallorca, and received a doctorate in theology there. He subsequently taught philosophy and theology at the same University. In 1749 he traveled to New Spain/Mexico, which had become a part of Spain's empire in 1521, to fulfill a life-long desire to serve the indigenous peoples of the New World. He was assigned to the Franciscan College of San Fernando in Mexico City. His first missionary assignment was in the Sierra Gorda northeast of Querétaro in central Mexico. When the Jesuits were expelled from all Spanish possessions in 1767, the Franciscans were assigned to take over most of the existing Jesuit missions. Father Serra was given the leadership over the 14 missions of Baja (Lower) California in 1768. In 1769 at the age of 56, Serra joined the expedition of Gaspar de Portolà to begin the settlement of Alta (Upper) California.

Juan Rodríguez Cabrillo had charted the coast of California for Spain in 1542. Although Spain had claimed Alta California as its territory by 1602, no concerted effort had been made to develop and settle this territory until the expedition of 1769. Since other countries such as France, Russia and England were also making New World claims and eyeing unoccupied territories, Spain felt the need to secure this region for itself through occupation. They would do this through the development of the mission system they knew so well from their experiences throughout the world. Additionally, a harbor along the Pacific coast would provide support to the ships supplying goods to the missions as well as to the Manila Galleons returning from China and the Philippines. Serra's role was to build the mission system in Alta California, serving the dual role of Christianizing the natives and preparing them for colonial development.

Serra founded the first nine missions in his 14 years in Alta California and was the *Presidente* of the Alta California mission system. Ultimately, there were 21 California missions. Carmel Mission (1771), the second of the missions he personally began, became the headquarters of the mission system and Serra's home. Serra died in 1784, at the age of 71, in his room at the Carmel Mission. He was buried at the altar of the existing adobe church until the stone church was completed in 1797, when he was re-interred at the altar where his body remains today. The stone basilica is the seventh and final church on this property.

When Mexico, originally called New Spain, won its independence from Spain in 1821, Alta California, which had belonged to Spain for over 200 years, became a part of the new Republic of Mexico. Mexico secularized and closed the missions in 1834, no longer needing them to continue colonial development. By that time, about 4,000 baptisms had been recorded at Carmel Mission. Once the missions were closed and no longer functioning as active parishes, many fell into disrepair due to a lack of funds for maintenance and conservation.

After 27 years as part of the Republic of Mexico, the United States obtained Alta California from Mexico in the Treaty of Hidalgo Guadalupe in 1848, ending the war between the two nations. The boundaries of the California we know today were not settled until 1849 in preparation for the state of California's entry into the United States in 1850.

By the 1880s, the Carmel Mission was significantly damaged. Most of its art and sculpture had been removed long before this time for safekeeping, but the physical structure was in danger of complete collapse. A fundraising effort was begun in the 1880s to re-roof the mission church to preserve it from disappearing altogether. Jane and Leland Stanford, founders of Stanford University, were essential donors and helped spearhead a campaign of fundraising to preserve the mission. The next generation of restoration began in the 1930s when Harry Downie was hired to start a process of complete restoration. Harry Downie led the restoration of Carmel Mission for over 50 years. He was knighted by the Church for this great, life-long endeavor and is buried in the historical graveyard on the north side of the Church. Harry Downie was responsible for researching and obtaining many of the original items that had graced the stone church from the late 1700s to secularization in 1834. Using church records and following leads and stories from descendants of original settlers and natives, Downie achieved the goal of bringing back to life this historic structure and its art collection.

The church was elevated to the status of a basilica in 1961 due to its historic and architectural significance, and Pope John Paul II visited the Carmel Mission in 1987.

Father John Griffin, the current pastor at Carmel Mission, has been an avid preservationist of the art collection, finding ways and means to accomplish expensive restoration to both statues and paintings. We hope you share our pride in the restoration and preservation of the historic art collection that was begun by Father Serra and which played an important role in early mission life in Alta California.

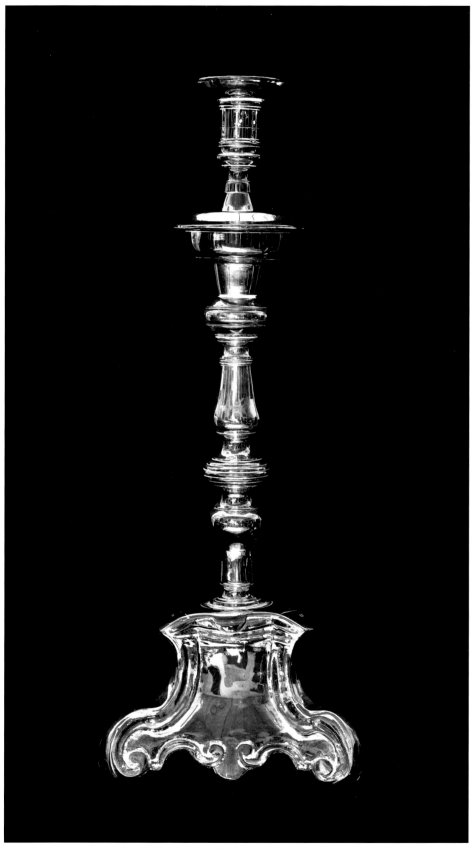

Main Altar Candlestick

MISSION ART

In 1767, the Franciscans were enlisted by the government of Spain to join the expedition that would help settle the new territory of Alta California and to build the mission system which Father Junípero Serra would lead. Based on their experiences working throughout the Americas and the Philippines, the Padres knew that paintings and sculpture were essential aids in helping the indigenous people understand and relate to the central figures and concepts of Christianity. Therefore, Father Serra began to order paintings and sculpture almost immediately for the future Alta California missions. A document from 1769, relating to the outfitting of the new missions, indicates that, in addition to the usual quantities of the customary vestments and silver, "seven sculptures of saints . . ." and "thirteen paintings" were to be placed on the ships bound for the new missions. This is indicative of how very important art was to missionary endeavors even during their first years of existence.

Spain's empire building created a significant demand for religious art, and the Catholic Church was the predominant art patron. The Church determined themes and content for artists. Art works of various kinds were shipped from Spain to the Americas and the Philippines and included many prints. Led by Spanish, Flemish and Italian artists, the indigenous people of Mexico learned to copy these prints precisely to represent God, the saints and key concepts of Christianity's beliefs and history. Thus began the religious art industry in the New World. The first painters' guild in Mexico was established in 1557 and developed and maintained artistic standards until 1785 when the Royal Academy of San Carlos was founded. The Academy introduced an official kind of neoclassicism and significantly eroded the guild system.

Apart from their obvious devotional and decorative value, paintings and sculpture played a significant instructional role in mission work. They served as tools for communicating powerful spiritual ideas to the native peoples who were converting to Christianity. Visual images were essential to the process of religious instruction because the friars' ability to use complex language in explaining religious ideas and theology was limited due to the variety of native languages of the new converts.

By 1785, the Church had opted for neoclassical simplicity rather than the Baroque style that had been dominant up to that time for works of art. This shift in style was in large part a royal decision and state policy. Prior to becoming king of the Spanish Empire, Charles III had been king of Naples where he was profoundly influenced by the classical style in the art and architecture being unearthed at that time in Pompeii, Italy. He mandated changes to artistic style in painting, sculpture and architecture. In fact, many Baroque-style buildings in Spain were renovated to remove or minimize Baroque elements and foster the neoclassical look. Some of the Carmel Mission art reflects this neoclassical simplicity.

With a two hundred year artistic tradition established in Mexico, Serra had many fine workshops and Mexican artists from which to select works for shipment to Alta California. The Franciscans also inherited the majority of the Baja California missions and the artworks found in those missions, some of which they took to the California missions. Only a master artist, as determined by the guild or academy, could sign a work. Since many of the mission works lack a signature, multiple artists-in-training could have contributed to a particular piece under the tutelage of a master. Because the demand for art was so large, workshops undoubtedly used their students in this manner to accommodate the range of requests they had to fill from the missions.

The Carmel Mission offers a significant representation of works from the Spanish Colonial period. This catalog highlights several that are on display throughout the Mission, particularly in the Basilica. Most pieces are original to the Mission. Some are of a later period but important to the Mission's history.

BASILICA

The Reredos   West wall, behind altar (illust. page 22)
The Reredos Crucifixion Scene   Above altar (illust. page 26)
The Five Statues of the Reredos   In reredos (illust. page 29)
The Glory of Heaven Painting   Sanctuary, south wall (illust. page 34)
Our Lady of Sorrows Painting   Sanctuary, north wall (illust. page 38)
The Serra Icon   Sanctuary, over Serra's grave (illust. page 40)
Statue of St. Joseph with Child Jesus   South wall (illust. page 42)
Statue of St. Francis Assisi   Sanctuary, south wall (illust. page 44)
Junípero Serra in Monterey Painting   North wall (illust. page 46)
The Stations of the Cross Paintings   Fourteen paintings, beginning along north wall near pulpit, continuing down and around south wall (illust. page 48)
The Virgin of Guadalupe Painting   North wall (illust. page 55)
St. Rose of Lima Painting   South wall (illust. page 58)
St. Isidore Painting   South wall (illust. page 60)
St. James, Santiago Painting   South wall (illust. page 62)
Our Lady of Belén Statue   Bethlehem Chapel (illust. page 64)
St. Anna, Mother of Virgin Mary Painting   Baptistry (illust. page 66)
Baptism of Jesus by John the Baptist Painting   Baptistry (illust. page 68)
The Crucifixion Scene Tableau   Passageway, near vestment room (illust. page 70)
Vestments   Passageway (illust. page 72)

MORA CHAPEL

The Junípero Serra Memorial Cenotaph   (illust. page 76)
Silver Bucarelli Monstrance   Chapel altar (illust. page 80)
Silver Chalice   Chapel altar (illust. page 82)
Silver Prayer Cards   Chapel altar (illust. page 84)
Silver Asperges Bucket   Floor in front of altar (illust. page 86)

PADRES' MUSEUM

Divine Shepherdess Painting   Serra Library (illust. page 88)
Virgin of Light Painting   Serra Library (illust. page 90)
Founding Painting   Museum hall (illust. page 92)
Zacatecas Sketch of Serra   Museum hall (illust. back cover)

SEASONAL PAINTINGS

(Locations vary with liturgical seasons, when displayed, are seen in the Basilica or Mora Chapel.)
The Visitation (illust. page 96)
The Awaking of the Apostles in Gethsemane (illust. page 98)

THE REREDOS

Harry Downie, Carmel, California, USA, 1956, redwood painted and gilded, 32' x 26'6"

Harry Downie, resident curator (1930–1980) for the restoration of Mission Carmel, finished a labor of love and installed this magnificent reredos, pronounced rĕr ĭ dŏs, in 1956. A reredos is a back piece, usually made of wood, complimenting the altar and decorating the back wall of a sanctuary. This reredos is an approximate replica of the original imported Mexican reredos which was installed in 1807 but destroyed in 1851 when the roof of the Mission collapsed. Because there were no known renderings of the original, Downie designed the reredos after reading diaries and descriptions written by padres and early visitors. He also travelled to Mexico studying church reredos and finally used the reredos of Mission Dolores in San Francisco as a guide. Built over seven months in 1956, it is composed of seventeen, painted and gilded, redwood sections, which were fitted together at the time of installation.

The beauty of the reredos lies in its color and form, accented by golden highlights, and the niches holding five statues of those especially venerated by the Franciscan mission founders. Under the patronage of these five saints are the names of five other California missions. A fuller description of these statues can be found in this catalog on page 29. Beginning at bottom left and moving clockwise, the five wood carved statues date from late 1700s to the early 1800s and are from Mexico:

1. *The Immaculate Conception* (*La Purisima Concepción*), mother of Jesus.
2. *Michael, the Archangel* (*San Miguel*), protector of the faith.
3. *St. Charles Borromeo* (*San Carlos*), patron saint of Carmel Mission.
4. *St. Anthony of Padua* (*San Antonio*), Franciscan priest and great preacher.
5. *St. Bonaventure* (*San Bonaventura*), cardinal and a Minister General of the Franciscan Order.

Atop the reredos is a carved, silver dove representing the Holy Spirit. Below the dove are two medallions, busts of St. Peter and St. Paul, purchased by Harry Downie in 1956 from a Carmel antique store. The carvings are attached to oval, scrolled bases. The artist and origin are unknown. The carving of St. Peter depicts him garbed in red with a light brown cloak over his shoulders. He appears the older of the two. His hair is wavy and he has a mustache and short beard. St. Paul appears wearing a gold garment and red cloak, and his hair and beard are longer. Below the medallion of St. Peter, the first pope, is a carved key. A book is carved

below the medallion of St. Paul, as the author of many Letters in the New Testament.

The centerpiece of the reredos is the modern, gilt bronze tabernacle behind a sheer golden curtain. It was purchased in Ireland and donated to the Mission in 1956. It houses the Eucharistic Hosts. Above the tabernacle stands the great cross with the corpus of Christ. Flanking the crucifix is the mother of Jesus and St. John the Apostle. This scene is described separately in the catalog on page 26.

Six Mexican candlesticks of the 1700s were brought by Father Serra to the Mission. Of a stately Renaissance design, the decorative, tripod bases are chased with spiral scrolls. They are 24 inches in height. The high-quality bronze was silver-plated in the 1960s with 16 pounds of pure silver. Candles are lighted for reverance and festiveness. Three are placed on each side of the altar representing the Trinity of God: Father, Son and Holy Spirit. Silver-plated over brass reflectors are often placed behind the candlesticks for special occasions.

At the time of the summer solstice and on a clear morning, a spectacular event occurs. The sun rises in the east, pouring its light through the star window on the façade of the Basilica. The light travels from left to right in a span of approximately twelve minutes, spotlighting the golden tabernacle in full glory. This solstice event is recorded in other Franciscan churches where this solar geometry and architecture have been incorporated in the original design. This event is recorded in this photo of the reredos.

Carmel Mission Summer Solstice, 2007

THE FIVE STATUES OF THE REREDOS

Anonymous, Mexico, circa 1770, wood, polychromed and gilded, 44" to 60"

THE IMMACULATE CONCEPTION

Mary, the Mother of Jesus, is in the lower left niche of the reredos. The title, *The Immaculate Conception* (*La Purisima Concepción*), refers to the doctrine that Mary was preserved from all sin from the moment of her conception. Standing upon a cloud with her hands in a prayerful position and no veil covering her face, Mary has a youthful appearance. Her garments look windblown around her exhibiting her majesty, her holiness as the one chosen by God to be the mother of the Savior. An overlay of silver has been applied to colored glazes giving an overall shimmering and fluid effect. This statue is not original to the Carmel Mission.

The provenance of the statue is vague, but it is known that Father Casanova, pastor of the Royal Presidio Chapel in Monterey, acquired it in the late nineteenth century. It was Harry Downie, curator and restorer of the Carmel Mission from 1930 to 1980, who brought it to reside here circa 1940.

Because of her importance as the mother of Jesus, Mary is honored under several titles. These feast days occur during the year with special Masses and celebrations. The feast of the Immaculate Conception is on December 8.

Michael the Archangel stands above Mary in the reredos. In both Hebrew and Christian scriptures, angels play a role in bringing aid or profound announcements from God to mankind. The twin attributes of angels, whereby these spiritual beings are recognized, are wings and facial features. Wings represent their mode of being in many places without the physical limitations of humans. Faces express human emotions by which angels relate to mankind and are a guide to truth, safety, and finally, to God in eternal life. This visual imagery of angels was first used in Byzantine art around the fourth century.

Michael, as Defender of the Faith, is often depicted with a sword and in military garb. In this sculpture, Michael is clothed as a Roman warrior. He wears a pleated, silver skirt, a blue tunic decorated with gold stars, the sun and the moon. His belt is gold. A long red stole swirls around his shoulder depicting his swift and ready action. He wears the boots of a Roman soldier.

This statue is listed in the archives of the Carmel Mission as "gifts from the King …1809–1 wood fig S. Michael."

The Archangel Michael is considered Protector of the Church, and his feast day is celebrated with Archangels Gabriel and Raphael on September 29.

St. Charles Borromeo (1538–1584) is the patron
of the Carmel Mission. It is fitting, as in all
California missions, that an image of the patron
is traditionally placed in a center, top position
of honor. St. Charles, a cardinal and bishop of
Milan, Italy, was a respected papal diplomat and
politician, instrumental in the final deliberations
of the Council of Trent (1545–1563), which
defined Church doctrines. Receiving his doctorate
in civil and canon law from the University of Pavia,
Italy, in 1559, he became a great patron of learning.
He established the Vatican Academy for literary
work, and he founded and endowed a college
known today as Almo Collegio Borromeo located
in Pavia, Italy. He was crucial during the time of
the plague in 1576, consoling the sick and bury-
ing the dead, visiting neighborhoods where the
contagion raged and bringing counsel as well as
financial aid.

King Charles III reigned over all Spanish
territories at the time the Mission was founded.
As headquarters of the Alta California missions
and as an honor to the king, the Carmel Mission
was placed under the patronage of St. Charles
Borromeo.

St. Charles, in this carved wood statue, wears
a thin mustache and a short goatee. He holds an
iron crosier in his right hand while his left hand
is raised, pointing to heaven. His eyes are of glass.
The red cloak, lined in green, and the miter on
his head are attributes of a bishop. These are
conferred on bishops and abbots to remind them
of their pastoral care for those entrusted to them,
as well as the important tasks of tending to the
needy. So too, is the iron crosier, the staff he holds
as a shepherd of his people. A lace-edged white
surplice, a red belt and stole can be seen beneath
his cape which is clasped by the morse, a two-part
fastening device. His clothing is finely embellished
with a floral and leaf design created by the estofado
technique symbolizing the stature of bishop and
cardinal.

The statue is believed to be original to the
Mission, acquired by Junipero Serra around 1772.
Even during the secularization period of the missions, a priest from the Monterey church would
come to Carmel Mission to celebrate mass on the
feast day of St. Charles on November 4th.

The statue of St. Anthony of Padua (1195–1231) is in the top right niche. Born Fernando de Bulhões, in Portugal, St. Anthony entered religious life in Lisbon. As a Franciscan he moved to Italy, took the name Anthony and worked in Morocco and Italy. His body is buried in a chapel of the Padua Basilica dedicated to him. The walls surrounding his tomb hold hundreds of small silver memorials representing the many miracles attributed to him.

He is held in close esteem with St. Francis Assisi of whom he was an ardent follower. Father Serra venerated St. Anthony as his personal patron. Serra requested that his patron be honored in the Carmel Mission, and Blessed Serra is buried in the sanctuary of the Basilica. Therefore, it is quite appropriate that this statue has been placed in a niche of the Carmel reredos.

This carving of the beloved St. Anthony depicts a curly headed priest garbed in the Franciscan brown habit, which is accented by estofado on the cowl, sleeves and hem. The cord at the waist is traditional to the Franciscan Order. St. Anthony holds a wooden staff with four lilies of white glass, symbols of his purity. The statue of the baby Jesus is a separate piece, cast by Harry Downie from the baby Jesus held by the St. Joseph statue, residing on the sanctuary south wall. Traditionally statues and paintings of St. Anthony depict him holding the lily and the child Jesus. Legend tells that shortly before his death, a very ill Anthony was recuperating on the estate of a wealthy landowner near Padua. One night the owner of the estate observed a brilliant light emanating from Anthony's room. Quietly peering in, he observed Anthony miraculously holding the baby Jesus.

Because of his success as a very effective teacher, preacher and confessor, St. Anthony is often called upon when one experiences a loss, even of a material possession. This is due to the fact that in his lifetime St. Anthony brought many "lost souls" to God.

An invoice of 1771 describes a statue of St. Anthony, and inventories of 1809 and 1835 list a statue of St. Anthony. It is thought that this sculpture is the same as that on the invoice and inventories.

The feast day of St. Anthony is celebrated on June 13th.

ST BONAVENTURE

The statue of St. Bonaventure (1221–1274), of the Franciscan Order of priests and a cardinal of the church, is placed in the lower right niche. Legend tells that although his given name was Giovanni, it was St. Francis of Assisi who exclaimed, "*O buona ventura!*" in response to the pleading prayers of Giovanni's mother for her dangerously ill child. Or, perhaps, Francis was speaking of Giovanni's future greatness.

In St. Bonaventure's hand is a book, reflective of his doctoral degree conferred in Paris and his composition of a text on the life of St. Francis. His red mantle and headpiece are indicative of his role as a cardinal. Over his black cassock is a surplice, shimmering with a glazed gilt finish and ornamented with a wide lace border. His eyes, as in the other statues, are of glass.

This statue is thought to be original to the Carmel Mission, although it is not located in an inventory until 1834. Its appearance is quite similar to the statues of Archangel Michael, St. Charles and St. Anthony. It could have been requested by Father Serra as part of a set of statues.

St. Bonaventure's feast day is July 15.

Before the Mission fell into disrepair, these five statues were relocated to Monterey and various sites for safekeeping. Harry Downie restored them and returned them to their rightful place after the completion of the new reredos in 1956. In 2008–2010, these statues were professionally conserved and restored.

THE GLORY OF HEAVEN

José de Paez, Mexico City, Mexico, 1771–1772, oil on canvas, 61¼" x 77½" (following page)

The Glory of Heaven is one of the Mission's most important paintings. The artist, José de Paez, was a student of Miguel Cabrera, one of the leading master artists of the Spanish Colonial period. Paez became a prolific painter of religious works, maps, caste paintings and portraits. He emerged as an important painter in Mexico in the second half of the eighteenth century.

The work is signed along the bottom of the painting and indicates Mexico City as its place of origin, a mark of distinction. Mexico City was the hub of the art world in Mexico and had many fine workshops. The fact that it is signed is another mark of distinction since only master artists who had achieved a certain level of expertise and experience were allowed to sign their paintings.

Father Serra personally commissioned this painting in 1771 along with one entitled *The Horrors of Hell*. The order to San Fernando College, Mexico City, read, "2 canvases, 2 *varas* long, almost square but greater in length than in height, one representing Heaven and the other Hell and their value not to exceed 100 *pesos*."

When the paintings were completed, they were shipped on the *Santiago* and arrived in Monterey on May 9, 1774, and recorded in Serra's 1774 *Informe* for Mission Carmel.

This painting is a good example of efforts to make the afterlife tangible. One of the core themes of religious paintings of the period was that heaven was open to all peoples who believed in God. Additionally, one of the sub-themes of many of the religious paintings was that the Church would unify all peoples—the religious, peasants, nobility, all of whom are represented in this painting. The painting of hell had all types of people and levels of society represented as well, thus making the point that God would be the final judge of mankind and decide who would enter heaven or hell.

The Glory of Heaven features figures of both the New and Old Testaments as well as local figures. In the center of the painting is St. Michael, the Protector of the Church and Missions. He is shown with St. Gabriel the Archangel who is holding the lily, a symbol of the Annunciation. St. John the Baptist is shown with the staff and lamb. Abraham is shown with a rabbi's headgear, and Adam and Eve are also represented.

The Trinity is represented as three men: Christ in blue with a cross, God the Father in white with the globe and the Holy Spirit in red. The Trinity idea originated with the story of three visitors to Abraham (Genesis 18). The tradition of the Trinity as three identical men first appeared in a mosaic at the church of St. Maria Maggiore in Rome and dates to 430. Around the mid-late 1700s, the church deemed that the Trinity should be shown with a dove as the Holy Spirit. So, the fact that there are still three men in the painting helps date this painting and may indicate that the change in how the Trinity was to be represented had not yet reached Mexico at the time it was painted.

Also in the painting are the apostles St. Peter, St. Paul, St. Joseph and Mary, St. Anne and St. Joachim (the Virgin Mary's parents), which helped reinforce the idea of family and of family being reunited in heaven. Many others are represented in the work including native people in the lower right hand corner, conveying the idea that indigenous converts would also receive their equal reward in heaven.

This painting would have been a powerful teaching tool as well as a work for devotional meditations. During the mission period, similar paintings on this subject matter were made for at least three other missions, in San Juan Bautista, San Miguel and Santa Barbara.

OUR LADY OF SORROWS

Partial signature: Ma Rodriquez, Mexico, circa 1777, oil on canvas, 62" x 51"

Our Lady of Sorrows was the title given to the Virgin Mary to commemorate the suffering she experienced during her Son's life, and especially during his passion and death on the cross. The painting focuses on the emotional moment at which Jesus has just been taken down from the cross. The climax of Christ's life is described in all four Gospels and attested to by Roman documents. In Christian doctrine, it is considered to be the ultimate sacrificial act, God allowing his son to die in atonement for human sin.

In the painting, Mary is shown in a red tunic, which symbolizes her intense devotion and love for Jesus. The blue mantle represents heaven. Her left hand extends towards heaven asking for God's intercession. Her right hand is over her heart showing her grief and sorrow while her eyes are cast upward.

Saint John the Apostle, one of Jesus' first apostles, was considered his favorite. Scripture relates he was present at most of Christ's important moments such as the miracle of the fishes and loaves, the transfiguration and the agony in the garden. He remained at the foot of the Cross until the very end when Christ was removed, as shown in the painting. One of John's attributes is a book, which is depicted at the bottom left of the painting. Saint John became the protector of Mary after Christ's death and subsequent resurrection. They moved to Ephesus where John and Saint Peter continued to work together.

The second woman in the painting is Mary Magdalene. Her attribute is the ointment jar shown at the bottom of the painting. She used oil on Jesus after washing his feet in repentance for her sins.

Jesus, the central figure, is draped with a white shroud. The wound in his side is barely visible, but the left hand and foot clearly show where the nails were driven. The crown of thorns and the used nails are carefully placed at his feet. The left arm and chest depict trauma. His head is resting on his distended chest as he is cradled by his Mother.

None of the figures are looking directly at Jesus. Rather, they avert their eyes from the tragedy that had unfolded. The pallor and immobility of Christ is contrasted by the dark figures of those who surround him. The illumination is coming from above, a heavenly light that appears to be shining on Christ's body and on the faces and hands of the others. The use of light and dark tones gives drama to the painting. This is called chiaroscuro. The dark recesses outline the forms and give them dimension and realism. The composition is tight and compact.

In 1778, Father Serra wrote from the Carmel Mission, "improvement . . . in the Church, there has been hung a beautiful painting of Our Lady of Sorrows seated at the foot of the Cross with her Divine Son laid on her lap." Aside from this notation in the inventory, little else is known about this painting. By virtue of the date entered in the inventory, we know that it was painted before 1777.

There is a partial signature, "Ma Rodriquez", however, nothing is known of the artist. The painting was originally larger, but it is believed that it had been damaged. In 1932, Harry Downie reduced the length of the painting by three inches, perhaps eliminating damage, and had it reframed in an existing original mission frame that is believed to have been made at the request of Father Serra for some other painting.

THE SERRA ICON

Brother Claude Lane, OSB, Oregon, USA, 2008, acrylic on wood, 22$\frac{1}{2}$" x 16"

This work of art is located over the grave of Father Junípero Serra at the foot of the altar in the Carmel Mission Basilica. To the left of his grave and icon are the graves of Fathers Crespi and Lopez. To the right is the grave of Father Lasuén who was the Alta California mission system's second *presidente*. This contemporary-styled icon was commissioned by the Carmel Mission and "written" by the artist. Written is the term used for preparing to create an icon by initially discerning the nature of the subject matter. A preliminary drawing is then made and from that, the final icon. The *Serra Icon* was produced by Brother Claude Lane, a Benedictine monk, at Mount Angel Abbey in the Willamette Valley of Oregon.

This image was based on a portrait of Father Serra painted by Andres Caymari, 1790. Brother Claude extrapolated from this portrait and re-imagined the stylized face that is shown in the icon. Serra is shown with a stole over his robe. The stole signifies that he was an ordained priest. The stole is red in color and follows the Baroque decoration of the period. Brother Claude also felt that because of Serra's many hardships, including the fact that he suffered from a leg ailment all his life, that red, being the traditional color for passion, would be an appropriate color for Serra's stole. One of Serra's hands is raised up with the fingers crossed as if making an "x" while also forming an "i" and a "c". Members of religious orders often used this symbol. The fingers are making the letters "ICXC" which are the Greek initials for the name of Jesus Christ.

Serra's head is bent to one side creating a sense of the gentleness for which he was known during his lifetime. He is holding the traditional Franciscan cross that was found around his neck when his tomb was opened. The robe is grey in color, common during Serra's time, but shadowed with brown tones, since contemporary Franciscans wear the brown robe. A 23-carat gold leaf halo surrounds his head. Gold is the traditional symbol for light and the heavenly realm. On one side of the halo are the words "Bl. Junípero" and on the other side "Serra."

The icon is painted on 1/2 inch thick birch wood. Birch is used because it is a tight, lightweight grain. The icon is painted in natural pigment acrylic paints made from authentic minerals, rather than paints made from chemicals in a lab. The icon is varnished to prevent cracking.

Brother Claude Lane is a well know iconographer. He entered Mount Angel Abbey in 1972 and made his vows in 1974 at the age of twenty-one. Since his childhood, Brother Claude had done many drawings and paintings, and so he was encouraged to try the art of iconography by Abbot Bonaventura in 1985. He became Mount Angel's full time iconographer in 1991. Brother Claude has written over one hundred icons and draws heavily from both Roman Catholic and Orthodox concepts. Unlike most iconographers who exactly copy outlines provided by ancient tradition, he prefers to follow the style of classic iconography while creating original images from multiple sources of inspiration.

ST. JOSEPH WITH CHILD JESUS

Anonymous, Mexico, mid 17th century, wood, polycromed and gilded, 35"h

On November 6, 1768, the *Visidor-General* of New Spain, José Galvez, proclaimed St. Joseph to be patron of the "Sacred Expedition" occupying Alta California. As husband of Mary and guardian of the child Jesus, St. Joseph would also be protector of the native Americans who were often considered children in the eyes of the padres. Each mission was to have one good representation of St. Joseph. This carving was originally placed in a gilt wooden niche with glass. Today it stands in a small, antique shrine inside the sanctuary.

The carving, painting and gold leaf application are of the highest quality. The folds of clothing were created by multiple layers of gesso and rabbit skin glue. The estofado technique was then used to create the leaf and vine design in the green robe and deep red cape. After the initial processes of preparing the wood, gold leaf was applied to achieve the desired design. Punch work and outlining of the design was accomplished with tools to create texture. Then multiple layers of paint and transparent glazes were placed on the sculpture, often covering the gold leaf. Ultimately the gold leaf design was revealed and redefined by delicately scratching away painted surfaces. To further embellish the gilt design, punches with various tips were applied to the gold leaf, creating depth, brilliance and dimension. This technique was also used on the statue of St. Francis. Though neither is signed, they possibly were created by the same artist or workshop.

A gold rope-like belt gathers the robe at St. Joseph's waist. His sandals are fashioned of thin brown thongs. The eyes are glass. Actual hair remains in the left eyelash, while the eyebrows exhibit fine brush work. The smaller size and fully finished backside indicate the statue could have been used in processions.

Images of St. Joseph are often depicted with lilies, and the five glass lilies decorating the staff are a nineteenth century addition. The infant, clothed in white lace, is separately carved and could be original. The ornate antique altar piece, encasing the statue, is embellished with gold leaf. This niche, not the original, was a donation in the late 1800s of Maria Antonia Field of the prominent Munras family of Monterey.

In a 1774 diary, Serra wrote, "… this Mission has had the following … additions to the Church and Sacristy … a niche more than 2 *varas* high with its *entral* cupola of redwood for the holy image of St. Joseph." Though mission secularization occurred in 1834, the statue remained in the sanctuary until abandonment of the church. Taken to the Royal Presidio Chapel in Monterey, it remained there until the 1930s restoration of the Mission.

THE STATUE OF SAINT FRANCIS ASSISI

Anonymous, Mexico, late 17th century, wood, polychromed and gilded, 60"h

St. Francis of Assisi (1182–1226) is one of the best loved and most frequently portrayed saints in ecclesiastical art. He is most often depicted wearing a brown robe with double rope cincture on which there are three knots representing the three Franciscan vows. Often he is portrayed with birds, a wolf or other animals because of his love of nature. Father Serra and members of the Franciscan community helped found California, and it is appropriate that California missions bring honor to St. Francis.

Born in the Italian town of Assisi, Francis gave up a life of worldliness and wealth at age 25 to dedicate his life to God. In his time, Francis was a radical who embraced non-violence, the sick, the poor, and all creation of God as holy. He sought simply to live out the teachings of Jesus. His Order of St. Francis was approved by Pope Innocent III in 1209. Its principal vows are poverty, chastity and obedience. A chief attribute of the Franciscans is humility.

St. Francis is also known for creating the first reenactments of the birth of Jesus in which living people and animals depict the birth of Christ on Christmas Eve. Subsequently, the making of Christmas crèches became popular.

This almost life-sized figure of St. Francis holding the cross of Christ is a Mexican work of wood. Because of its size, the statue was created by several pieces of wood, clamped together. Multiple layers of gesso were applied and sanded down, forming the curves and shape of the clothing. The palm tree design was meticulously created by an artisan's handwork using the estofado technique, described in the essay about the St. Joseph statue. The technique was used in ancient cultures and refined by fifteenth and sixteenth century artists. Looking carefully, one might see the punch work or "tooling" on the gold that contributes to the intricate design.

The face is beautifully carved with emotion expressed in his sorrowful eyes, the upturned brows and slightly opened mouth. The brown eyes are of glass. His nose is prominent with a high and sensitive ridge, and his hair is closely cropped in typical monastic style. His slender neck is encircled by the hood and cowl of his brown robe. The stigmata, which are the wound marks in similar positions as those of the crucified Christ, is evident on his hands. The addition of the crucifix, of Italian wood and plaster, was made in 1976.

The statue has had an active history. It was carved in Mexico for the Santa Cruz Mission circa 1790. An earthquake occurred in that area in 1854, causing the collapse of that church and damage to the statue. Retrieved and temporarily placed in a Franciscan orphanage in Watsonville, California, the statue was later placed in Santa Barbara Mission Cemetery until 1972. Harry Downie, chief restorer from 1930 to 1980, was able to trade Chumash Indian baskets for the St. Francis statue. Restored in the 1970s and again in 2008, the carving is set on a gilded pedestal. It holds historical and sentimental significance residing near the place of Father Serra's burial.

St. Francis' feast day is celebrated on October 4th, often with the blessing of pets and other animals in many churches.

detail of robe

JUNÍPERO SERRA IN MONTEREY

Leo (Leopold) Leinweber, California, USA, 1894, oil on canvas, 96" x 54"

This painting was commissioned in 1894 by the Native Sons of the Golden West for the Custom House in Monterey, which they leased from the Federal Government from about 1890–1930 and used as a lodge. When the California State Parks took over the building, the painting was considered to be too religious for a state building. In 1937, it was given to Carmel Mission, as the Mission was in the midst of renovation. The painting was hung in Crespi Hall on the Mission grounds until it was cleaned and relined in 2004 and then moved into the Basilica. Today it hangs over a reliquary holding pieces of Father Serra's original coffin.

In this painting, Father Serra is a near life-size figure dressed in a gray-brown habit secured by a cincture on which his rosary is fixed. His right hand holds a crucifix aloft. The crucifix has an irregular, filmy gray covering on the lower portion of Christ's body. Serra is standing on a level grassy area with scattered boulders, flowers and gray-green vegetation. In the background lie two large rock formations with the Monterey Bay behind and the mountains across the water. The sky is muted pink and gray, suggesting early morning.

The artist, Leo (Leopold) Leinweber, was born in Hamburg, Germany, on October 11, 1861. He died on December 18, 1909. He was a painter, sculptor and engraver. From 1879–1885, he studied at academies in Munich and Berlin. During his studies he traveled to France, Italy, Switzerland and California. Leinweber may have been in California to participate in the 1894 California International Fair held in Golden Gate Park. This may explain how he came to obtain the commission.

THE STATIONS OF THE CROSS

José María Uriarte, Mexico, circa 1802, oil on canvas, a set of 14, 42" x 34" each

In Catholic churches everywhere, the Stations of the Cross grace the walls. The stations constitute 14 events of Jesus' journey to his crucifixion. Represented in the catalog are six images of the Mission's set of stations. They are Station I, *Jesus is Condemned to Death*; Station VI, *Veronica Wipes the Face of Jesus*; Station VII, *Jesus Falls the Second Time*; Station X, *Jesus is Stripped of His Garments*; Station XII, *Jesus is Raised Upon the Cross and Dies*; Station XIV, *Jesus is Laid in the Sepulchre*.

The Stations of the Cross date from 1802 and were painted by José María Uriarte. Uriarte was an active, well-known painter by 1813. After Mexican independence in 1821, Uriarte became the director of the new "School of Fine Arts" within the Institute of Sciences in Guadalajara, Mexico, where he remained until 1835. His main surviving work is a suite of 17 oval paintings and other works in the Cathedral of Guadalajara which date from about 1828–1835.

Kurt Baer, former art historian of the California missions, indicated the date of 1802 for receipt of this collection of paintings, and that date also appears on the front of the 14th station along with Uriarte's name. These paintings would have arrived unframed at the mission and would have been framed at the time of receipt. They were reframed in 1856 by Juan Bonafacio, a local framer.

The stations were scientifically cleaned and restored during the 1990s through the generosity of Mr. William Karges, a Carmel fine arts gallery owner.

The Stations of the Cross were not in general use in Catholic churches until the end of the seventeenth century. The object of the Stations is to help the faithful make a spiritual pilgrimage to the chief scenes of Jesus' suffering and death in Jerusalem. Making the actual pilgrimage to Jerusalem was the goal of many pious pilgrims dating back to the days of Constantine.

As early as the fifth century, institutions outside of Jerusalem tried various ways to recreate the important shrines of Jesus' journey to the cross. It wasn't until the fifteenth century that any standards for the stations were more firmly established. The earliest use of the word "stations", as applied to Jesus' walk to the Cross, occurs in a narrative of an English pilgrim, William Wey, who visited the Holy Land in 1458 and 1462.

By the early part of the sixteenth century, several different types of reproductions of the holy places were being set up in various parts of Europe for devotional purposes. The number of stations varied. In 1686, Pope Innocent XI granted a request by the Franciscans to erect Stations in all their churches. In 1731, Pope Clement XII fixed the number of Stations at fourteen. Finally, in 1862, it was determined that the Stations could be erected in any church, not just those of the Franciscans, and they have since become a traditional part of every Catholic Church.

THE FIRST STATION

Jesus is Condemned to Death

THE SIXTH STATION
Veronica Wipes the Face of Jesus

THE SEVENTH STATION
Jesus Falls the Second Time

THE TENTH STATION

Jesus is Stripped of His Garments

THE TWELFTH STATION
Jesus is Raised Upon the Cross and Dies

THE FOURTEENTH STATION

Jesus is Laid in the Sepulchre

THE VIRGIN OF GUADALUPE

Anonymous, Mexico, early to mid-1800s, oil on canvas, 99" x 58" (following page)

The paintings done in the New World accentuated the cultural dimensions of their settings and peoples. *The Virgin of Guadalupe* is an excellent example of these cultural and artistic mergers.

The story of the Virgin of Guadalupe is familiar to many. In 1531 the Virgin appeared to Juan Diego on a hill at Tepeyac, just north of Mexico City, which was the former home of the Aztec mother-goddess "Tonantzin". The Virgin spoke to Diego in his native Aztec language of Nahuatl. Diego described her as being dark skinned with garments as brilliant as the sun. She asked him to build a church for her on that hill. Diego went to the Bishop who listened but wanted proof of the apparition. So, upon the next visitation of the Virgin to Diego, she told him to gather roses that were blooming out of season in December and give them to the Bishop while repeating her request. When Diego opened his cloak to give the roses to the Bishop, there were not only the roses, but an image of the Virgin as Diego had described her on the cloak. The Bishop built a church on the site, and eventually several other churches were built there as well.

By the 1600s, images of the apparition were being produced. The first known large scale copy of *Our Lady of Guadalupe* is dated 1606 and signed by the master painter Baltasar de Echave Orio, founder of one of the principal seventeenth century dynasties of painters in Mexico City.

In 1666 some painters were given an extraordinary opportunity to examine the relic cloth and they declared it miraculous and perfect. As a result of treatises written by Creole (Europeans born in Mexico) intellectuals and clerics, a campaign to legitimize the Virgin as the special patroness of Mexico began in the mid-1600s.

The miracle-working *Virgin of Guadalupe* flooded the world with medals, prints and devotional paintings. By 1688, almost every church in Mexico had an altar dedicated to the Virgin of Guadalupe, and her image was disseminated to Spain, Germany, Italy and France.

The Virgin appears with hands in a prayerful position. She is clothed with a brilliant garment and often within an oval body of scalloped clouds. A crescent moon is beneath her feet and a crown rests on her head. The cloak is covered with stars alleged to have aligned with the constellation on the date of one of her appearances to Juan Diego. The Carmel Mission painting shows several Latin inscriptions. A "mystic dialog" surrounds her image with six small vignettes depicting the story of her apparition.

In 1751, master painter Miguel Cabrera was given an opportunity to inspect the original image, and in 1752, he made three copies directly from the original. This painting was originally attributed to Cabrera in some of the mission records. However, curators from Mexico City's National Museum examined the painting and determined that this is not a Cabrera, and the artist remains unknown. In 1754 Pope Benedict XIV confirmed the Virgin of Guadalupe as patroness of Mexico. Juan Diego was canonized by Pope John II in 2002.

The Carmel Mission painting was likely done in the early to mid-1800s. It was acquired by Frances Elkins and David Adler on a trip to Mexico. They purchased it from an antiques dealer and then kept it folded in their attic or basement for years. In 1952 they brought it out of storage and offered it to Harry Downie. He was delighted and had it restored whereby the folds almost disappeared. It was professionally conserved in 1998 by William Karges, fine art gallery owner in Carmel, who underwrote the large expenditure.

detail of lower right

ST. ROSE OF LIMA

Anonymous, Mexico, circa 1770s, oil on canvas, 99" x 68½"

Rose of Lima (1586–1617) was born "Isabella" to Spanish immigrants in Lima, Peru. Rose was an extraordinarily reverent person from her childhood, and despite the opposition of her parents, she lived a life of prayer. She is known for her role as the founder of social work in Peru. Although ridiculed in her lifetime, Rose was believed to be a great mystic and visionary. She died at age 31 in Lima, and many miracles were attributed to her.

This oil painting shows a serene St. Rose of Lima kneeling and wearing a white robe. On her head is a crown of roses. A dark blue cape tops the white habit of the Dominican Order to which she was devoted. Angelic cherubs rise above her and are crowned with pink roses. Faintly pictured below her is an outdoor garden fence decorated with these similar, delicate roses. Though depicted in serenity and beauty, her life was probably a difficult one. *S. Rosa de Limá* is scripted on the lower portion of the original frame, constructed in the Mission workshop.

The provenance of this painting is obscure. It was created in a Mexican workshop, and its size and style are similar to three others considered original to Carmel Mission that hang in the Basilica. They are *St. Rose of Virterbo*, *Saint James the Greater* (*Santiago Apostol*) and *St. Isidore* (*S. Isidro Labrado* [sic]). However, the *St. Rose of Lima* painting is not recorded in early mission inventory documents, while the others are documented as being original to the Mission.

St. Rose was the first canonized saint of the Americas, officially brought into the calendar of church saints in 1671 by Pope Clement X. Because of Rose's importance in the New World, her image is often placed in churches, and she is frequently named as patron of churches in the western hemisphere.

She is patroness of gardeners and of the Order of Dominican Sisters. Her feast day is celebrated on August 30th.

ST. ISIDORE

Anonymous, Mexico, circa 1773, oil on canvas, 99" x 68½"

Prior to the establishment of the Carmel Mission, the small tribes of the Monterey Peninsula and Carmel Valley were hunters and gatherers. Later, as workers in the Mission fields, the natives learned farming skills of tilling soil, planting crops, harvesting and storing seeds and food. Thus, this large vertical painting of *St. Isidore* (1070–1130) would have resonated with the native Americans working at the Mission.

This simple painting is held in a Mission-made frame inscribed, *S. Isidro Labradro* (sic), in the lower center of the frame. It was on the estate of a wealthy landowner in Spain that Isidore worked his entire life. The manor is pictured atop a hillside in the background. Isidore holds the shovel representing his farming labors. He wears simple layered shirts, shortened pants and working boots. His jacket seems somewhat formal, not suited to a laborer in the field, and perhaps added to indicate his future importance as a result of his canonization.

There are several legends associated with Isidore. One story relates to Isidore's practice of attending daily Mass and, therefore, arriving to work somewhat later than the others. This resulted in complaints to the lord of the estate that Isidore wasn't doing his full share of the work. When the estate owner came to resolve the situation, he saw an angel helping Isidore complete his share of the work. In the painting, we see the angel driving the oxen through the fields. Another legend tells that because of Isidore's love of animals, he shared corn seed with the birds. Yet when he arrived back at the mill, his seed bag was still filled to the brim.

Of particular note is the date of canonization of St. Isidore and his wife Maria in 1622. The giant figures of St. Ignatius Loyola, St. Francis Xavier, St. Teresa of Avila and St. Philip Neri were all canonized on the same day as Isidore and Maria. Although the peasant Isidore left no writings, teachings or professed disciples, he was admired for his great charity to others and faithfulness to God. "In the list of canonized saints his type is rare: in heaven, presumably, not so," writes Robert Ellsberg in his book *All Saints*.

St. Isidore is appropriately the patron saint of farmers, and paintings of St. Isidore are hung in many rural churches. The celebration of St. Isidore is on May 15th.

ST. JAMES THE GREATER (SANTIAGO APOSTOL)

Unknown, Mexico, circa 1773, oil on canvas, 99" x 68½"

Known in Spain as *Santiago*, St. James the Greater is the patron saint of Spain. He was one of Jesus' twelve apostles, and he was the brother of John and son of Zebedee. After Christ's death, he went to Spain as a missionary. In this painting, he is pictured barefoot and with a staff and travelling bundle. His acorn-colored robe is topped with a green cape, fastened at his neck with two scalloped shells. A vivid red shawl swirls about him suggesting motion and his travels. The background hill and mountains are indicative of Spanish landscape.

In St. James' hand, he holds *Our Lady of the Pillar*, which refers to the first Marian apparition, about 40 A.D. to St. James in Zaragoza, Spain. Tradition holds that Mary, the mother of Jesus, told James that in difficulty she would appear to him, encouraging his work in Spain. In later years, a discouraged St. James received an apparition of Mary holding the child Jesus and standing on a column. She asked that a place of prayer be built. The chapel James built was the first ever to be dedicated to Mary, and eventually a large church was built. Despite invasions, bombs and wars, the Basilica built in 1681 still stands over the site of James' first chapel.

The shells are a reference to the shrine of Santiago de Compostela, a major pilgrim site near the western coast of Spain. It is believed to be the resting place of the body of St. James. Pilgrims who journey to the shrine wear a shell on their clothing or hats, signifying their journey to the coast. The shrine is most often approached, in some part or for many miles, on foot as a walking pilgrimage.

The painting's frame was made in a mission workshop. The words, *Santiago Apostol*, appear in painted script at the bottom of the frame. The large painting is one of a set that arrived in California about 1777, ordered by Father Serra during his visit to Mexico City a few years after the founding of the Carmel Mission. The paintings were probably rolled in a protective cover and then framed in the Mission workshop. Others in the set are *St. Isidore*, *St. Rose of Lima* and *St. Rose of Virterbo*, all hanging in the nave of the Basilica.

OUR LADY OF BELÉN

Anonymous, Mexico, circa 1770, polychromed wood with textile dress, 62"h

Devotion to our Lady of Belén dates back to the fifteenth century. Prince Henry the Navigator built a small chapel near Lisbon at Belem, Portugal, so that sailors might invoke the intercession of the Virgin Mary in conjunction with their voyages. Our Lady of Belén has been the patroness of sailors ever since.

The Mission's statue has a colorful history. The statue was named *La Conquistadora* and is one of the oldest statues in California. It was created in Mexico by an unknown artist and originally owned by the Bishop of Mexico, Francisco Antonio Lorenzana y Butrón. The Bishop gifted it to José de Galvez, *Visidor-General* of Mexico, who sent it on the ship *San Antonio* with Don Gaspar de Portolà, Governor and Commander of the expedition to Alta California. The ship left Acapulco in 1768. Father Serra was to use the statue in conjunction with the inauguration of each of the new missions. Our Lady of Belén was present at the founding of the first mission in San Diego in 1769. The statue arrived in Monterey in 1770 and was present at the celebration of the founding Mass there. Then, de Portolà was instructed by Serra to take the statue back to San Blas, Mexico, on his return trip because Father Serra mistakenly thought the statue was on loan to the missions. However, when de Portolà arrived in Mexico, he was told to leave the statue on the ship for the next trip to Alta California, for the Bishop's intent was that the statue remain there.

In 1798, Lieutenant Matute had a silver crown made for the statue with an inscription of thanksgiving for his safety during a difficult sea voyage. The crown is 12 inches high and 10 inches in diameter with the inscription in Spanish:

> "Out of devotion of Naval Lt. Don Juan Bautista Matute, commander of the frigate 'The Most Pure Conception.' He obtained relief. Dedicating the crown October of 1798."

Altars of all seven Carmel Mission churches have been graced with this statue. In 1797, Carmel Mission's seventh and last church, the present stone Basilica, was completed and *Our Lady of Belén* was placed on the altar.

By the time of the closure of the mission system in 1834, most of the art and sculpture had been given to other churches, hospitals, convents, orphanages or placed in storage. By 1842 the statue stopped appearing in the inventories. An Indian named Cantua, living at the Mission's Orchard House, had become the guardians of the statue. Dona Maria Ignacia Dutra, a daughter of the Cantuas, continued the guardianship of the statue. Upon Dutra's death in the 20th century, the statue was deeded to Tulita Westfall, a Boronda descendent. The Boronda family were early *Californios* who settled in the territory. Tulita moved to Oakland, California, taking the statue with her.

Armed with this information, Harry Downie located Tulita and the statue. Downie, hired to restore the Mission beginning in the 1930s, offered to make repairs to the statue and convinced Tulita to return the statue to the Mission. The statue was then placed in the former mortuary chapel, now referred to as Our Lady of Bethlehem Chapel. Downie made the large display case for the statue where it has remained since about 1948.

The clothed, life-size statue is of carved wood covered with a matte finish of several layers of extremely thin gesso achieving a porcelain-like sheen. The statue has the original wood face, hands and glass eyes. Harry Downie carved a wooden form for the body of the statue to replace the termite damaged original.

The original costume for the statue was lost over time. Downie procured the current dress from a Mexican antiques dealer. The silver embroidered dress was thought to be about 250 years old at the time of its purchase, probably sometime between 1940 and 1960. The gold acorn earrings were a family heirloom, believed to be some of the first jewelry made in California, from the Tulita Westfall family.

The crown had been kept over the tabernacle of the San Carlos Church in Monterey. Downie recovered the crown and returned it to the statue's head. The infant in Our Lady's arms is original and was also retrieved from San Carlos Church where it had been placed in the arms of a St. Joseph statue.

The display case has a silk background that had been ordered by Father Serra and is said to have come from Canton, China. The spiral columns of the display case came from South America, a gift of Noel Sullivan of Carmel (1894–1956) and nephew of California senator James Phelan.

SAINT ANNA, MOTHER OF BLESSED VIRGIN MARY

José de Paez, Mexico City, Mexico, circa mid-late 1700s, oil on canvas, 72" x 60"

According to Christian tradition, St. Anna was the Mother of the Virgin Mary, the Mother of Jesus. In the Gospel of James, dating back to the second century, we are told that Anna, wife of Joachim, was in advanced years and childless when she conceived Mary in answer to her prayers. St. Anna proclaimed she would dedicate this child to the service of God.

This painting represents the apparition of the angel to St. Anna telling her she would conceive a child. St. Anna is shown looking toward heaven with her hands clasped in prayer. She is wearing a gold colored robe over a green mantle with a red robe underneath. On her left side a single cherub looks down from above as two other cherubs appear over her right. She is standing near what appears to be a seawall with a body of water in the background.

The painting is signed by José de Paez, born in Mexico City around 1720 and thought to have died around 1790. He was considered a very fine painter and one of the most prolific artists of the Spanish Colonial period. Although he specialized in religious subjects, he showed equal skill in the execution of large scale works depicting daily life in Mexico with great and delicate detail. Another de Paez painting called *The Glory of Heaven* hangs in the sanctuary.

According to Mission records, this painting was received in 1978. It was purchased through art dealers for the Carmel Mission by the late Sam Stark of Pebble Beach. Whether this painting ever belonged to one of the California missions before 1978 is unclear. The painting has undergone some conservation in the past and is in fair condition. It now hangs in a massive late-Victorian, gilt frame of gesso cast ornamentation over wood with highlights of water gilding.

St. Anna is the patron saint of Quebec. Her feast day is July 26th.

BAPTISM OF JESUS BY JOHN THE BAPTIST

Anonymous, Mexico, mid 17th century, oil on canvas, 36" x 24"

Although it has no signature, this Spanish Colonial work was painted by an artist who would have been acquainted with drawings of Renaissance paintings that had been brought to Mexico by the Franciscans. Its simplicity may remind one of works like Piero della Francesca's Baptism painting that today hangs in the National Gallery of London.

In this work, Jesus' clothing is held by an angel while he receives the waters with humility to signify his union with humanity. In a solemn expression of his privilege, John the Baptist pours water from the Jordan River with a scallop shell. The words seen lettered on the banner of the staff are "*Ecce Agnus Dei . . .*" meaning, "Behold the Lamb of God." Doves fly inward to this moment of importance, signalling the beginning of Jesus' public life. Egrets wade in the background. Two colorful birds rest in the tree to the left, and a rabbit is in the lower left.

There are significant differences to be noted in the halo shapes. God the Father has a triangular shape halo representing the Trinity. The halo of Jesus is spiked, perhaps indicating the crown of thorns placed on his head at the Crucifixion. John's halo is circular, a probable reference to his death. The narrative of Mark 6:14-29 tells of Herodias' daughter performing a pleasing dance for Herod. He sought to give her any gift that she desired, and she consulted her mother Herodias. The request was made for the head of John the Baptist, subsequently brought to her on a plate, complying with her request.

The painting takes references found in the Gospels of Matthew 3:13-17, Mark 1:9-11, Luke 3:21-22, and John 1:29-34. John writes that the Baptist saw Jesus coming toward him and said, "Behold, the Lamb of God, who takes away the sin of the world." Luke records, ". . . the holy Spirit descended upon him in bodily form like a dove. And a voice came from heaven, 'You are my beloved Son; with you I am well pleased.'"

The ancient words of Old Testament prophets, Isaiah and Malachi, forecasted hope that a messenger would prepare the way of the Lord. The Baptist's appearance in history records the fulfillment of these prophets.

THE CRUCIFIXION SHRINE TABLEAU

Manuel Chile (Caspicara), Ecuador, late 18th century, polychromed wood and textiles
heights vary from 16" x 39"

This four-piece, wood sculptured shrine was created by the indigenous artist, Manuel Chile (unknown-1792) of Quito, Ecuador. The noted sculptor is also known by the name Caspicara. In Quito, the beginning of art with European mode influence is attributed, in part, to a Dominican friar, Pedro Bedon (1556–1621). Caspicara was a student of Bernardo de Legarda, another noted Spanish Colonial artist. Caspicara's works are also found in the Museo de Arte Colonial, Ecuador's finest collection of sixteenth–eighteenth century colonial art, as well as in many Quito churches.

In this work, and according to Scripture, the crucified Christ is surrounded by his mother Mary, Mary Magdalene and the Apostle John. The body of Christ is the ashen color of death. The wounds, the veins and the bones of his body are realistically detailed. The fan-shaped, carved gold elements protruding from both sides of his head indicate extraordinary holiness.

The figure of Mary has an astounding presence in the grouping. She is robed in deep, rich-brown velvet. A cream colored lace neckpiece, above Mary's gown and cape, is embellished with fine golden embroidery. She wears the most elaborate and intricately carved of the silver aureoles, denoting her unique holiness. The immense sadness in her eyes of glass and the positioning of her outstretched arms and hands demonstrate the story of a mother in agony over the death of her son.

The figures of the other Mary and St. John are likewise deeply expressive in their facial features, eyes and hands. Their bodies are also wood sculpted, painted with beautiful estofado work, a technique of layering paint over gold, and later scratching the surface to show the gold. Delicate and detailed beauty is thus given to garments using this technique.

When President-elect Herbert Hoover and his wife Lou Henry of Monterey traveled the coast of South America by ship, this four-piece sculpted shrine was presented to Hoover. He would be inaugurated a month later in Washington D.C. as President of the United States. The Hoovers were graduates of Stanford University and gave this sculpture to their alma mater after his presidency. Harry Downie discovered it during his years restoring the Mission. As a fine example of Spanish Colonial art, Downie purchased it for the Mission.

It is of historical note that the Hoovers professed their marriage vows in the front courtyard of Carmel Mission.

LITURGICAL VESTMENTS

Anonymous, circa 18th–20th century, silk, cotton, velvet, metals, pearls, sizes vary, 43" to 47" x 23" to 32"

The vestment collection at the Mission includes chasubles, copes, stoles, chalice veils, and paten palls which are also called burses. The chasuble is the outermost vestment the priest wears in the celebration of the Mass. Copes are worn in processions and special occasions. Stoles are worn over the shoulders. Chalice veils cover the chalice, and burses are fabric envelopes to hold the paten, the plate which covers the chalice.

The chasuble originates from the common outer traveling garment, a *casula*, of the late Roman Empire. Translated as "little house," this poncho-like covering was also used by peasants working in the fields. It is uncertain when this covering became a liturgical garment, but we learn from mosaics and paintings that chasubles were worn in Italy by the clergy as early as the sixth century. In 742, a decree was issued that the chasuble was to be worn by the clergy during Mass.

The style of the chasuble evolved during the centuries that followed. From the thirteenth century, practicality dictated a more fluid garment, free of bulk. Originally the chasuble had full sleeves. Later the sleeves were cut open, and finally sleeves were eliminated or undefined. The dalmatic style had sleeves and could be worn by a deacon. Lengths were shortened. In the collection is one style called "fiddle back." This particular type of vestment is of the kind that would have been worn by Father Serra at the Mission.

Complex decorative schemes and embellishments were used in the making of vestments which included images of the cross, the Y-shaped cross, Christ, Mary, the saints and liturgical symbols. Rich silk and brocade fabrics were embellished with decorative gold and silver threads, pearls, metals, beads and complex embroidery work. Often the decorative themes included grapes and wheat, symbolizing the bread and wine consecrated during the Mass. Birds and flowers were frequently used as symbolic features.

Baroque and Rococo influences are often evident in the decorative bands that hide the seams and strengthen stress points in the garments. Customary today is a simpler garment whose beauty depends on the material, form and drape rather than on elaborate decoration.

The color of the chasuble, stole and chalice veil depend upon the liturgical season or the celebratory rite. Green is used during Advent and Lent and many days of the year; white is used during the Christmas and Easter seasons, for feasts celebrating Mary and for weddings; red is used on Pentecost and for feast days of martyrs;

gold is sometimes used for very special celebratory days. In days past, black was the color worn for funerals; white is now sometimes used instead.

The earliest liturgical garments were brought to the New World from Spain where silk weaving centers had developed from the time of the Islamic invasions of 710 A.D. Guilds for weavers, designers and embroiderers resulted in fine vestments. In Mexico, textile industries in Mexico City, Puebla and Querétaro produced designs, combining indigenous and Spanish elements with luxurious Asian silks and brocades. Although not all were so richly decorated, these magnificent vestments were produced by unknown designers, weavers, and artisans from Mexican and European workshops. Their origins are thought to be eighteenth–twentieth century.

detail of a vestment

Fiddle Back Chasuble

Funeral Chasuble

Dalmatic Chasuble

JUNÍPERO SERRA MEMORIAL CENOTAPH

Joseph (Jo) Jacinto Mora, California, USA, 1924, bronze on marble base, 144" x 99"

This cenotaph was created by Joseph Jacinto (Jo) Mora from 1920–1924 at the request of Father Raymond Mestres, pastor of San Carlos Church in Monterey, as a monument and tribute to Father Serra. Originally to be located in the Mission Church as a sarcophagus with the remains of Serra, it was soon realized to be too large for placement in the sanctuary. It was then decided that a small chapel would be built adjacent to the Basilica to contain the sculpture, which would instead be a cenotaph, containing no body. The cenotaph was unveiled in October, 1924. The chapel became the first phase of the reconstruction of the padre's living quarters, now the Padres Museum at Carmel Mission.

Joseph Jacinto Mora (1876–1947) was born in Uruguay and was the son of Catalan sculptor Domingo Mora and a French mother named Laura Guillard. The family moved to New England when Jo was an infant. He studied art and worked as an illustrator in Boston. But he spent the majority of his life in the west, painting western scenes with cowboys and native Indians. He traveled from mission to mission on horseback in California, painting the missions in his sketch book and creating his famous illustrated maps. He then assisted his father in their sculpture studio in San Francisco. In 1920 he moved to Carmel to work on the Serra cenotaph where he remained until his death in 1947.

The bronze sculpture sits on a base of travertine. The artist features Father Serra as he was prepared for burial, clothed in a Franciscan habit with a stole, crucifix, cord and rosary. His bare feet rest on a bear cub, a symbol of the state of California. Father Juan Crespi, life-sized and bending forward, stands at Father Serra's head. He was Father Serra's closest associate and came with him on the Gaspar de Portolà expedition from Baja California to Alta California in 1769. Father Fermin Lasuén kneels at Serra's feet on the left. He became Serra's successor as the next *Presidente* of the mission system. Father Julian Lopez kneels

at the right foot. He was a young friar who died at the Mission. All three were eventually buried beside Father Serra in the sanctuary of the Basilica near the altar.

The base support of the cenotaph has four insert carvings of three figures each: Franciscan friars, Spanish soldiers, Indian converts and non-converted Indians. Between these inserts are medallions of Pope Pius VI and King Carlos IV of Spain who ruled at the time Serra died.

A bronze frieze around the main sculpture describes several notable events in early mission history. Three panels on the left describe Father Serra and expedition leader Gaspar de Portolà with a body servant and bugler, a squadron of Spanish cavalry, leather jacketed light cavalrymen and a pack train transporting goods from mission to mission. The three panels on the right represent an attack at San Diego mission by Indians, the first Mass of Father Serra in Monterey and the first baptism at Carmel Mission.

The brass inscription around the top translates:

"Junípero Serra, the legitimate son of Antonio Serra and Margarita Ferrer. He was born in Petra, the island of Mallorca, Spain on the 24th of November 1713. He was clothed in the Franciscan habit on the 15th of September 1737. He embarked for the missions of Mexico in 1749. He was the President of the nine missions in Alta California. This work was devised and carried out by Rev. Ramon Mestres, and originated and executed in 1924 by the sculptor, Jo Mora. Both patricians of the V.P. President, who died here in 1784. RIP."

Ornate metal molding around the entire cenotaph illustrates the benefits that California received from the Spanish missions, which included fruit, grain and livestock. On the foot of the cenotaph is a cartouche of Spain's royal coat of arms with a Franciscan cord and California poppies draped over it.

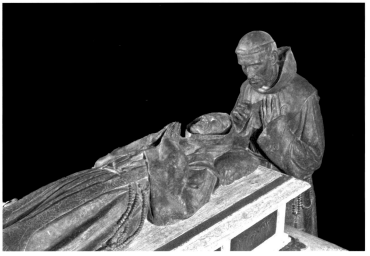

detail

detail

detail

detail

detail

From the early 1500s, the Spanish were mining the rich silver lodes of Mexico. Silversmith shops were established and became beehives of activity for the purpose of making vessels and altar furnishings for the Mass.

The Carmel Mission silver includes Baroque styled objects first brought by the Jesuits to their missions in Baja California. In 1785, the simplicity of the neoclassic style was introduced into all art, including the making of silver. But the fluid forms and intricate details of the Baroque style were not easily replaced.

It should be said that not all Mexican silver made in past centuries is stamped with the markings required by the government. This, however, does not indicate that unmarked silver pieces are not valuable or even authentic. Many of the Mission's silver pieces have markings. From 1638–1732, an eagle tax stamp and an artisan's mark were required. From 1733–1782, an added chief assayer mark was required to signify the metal was of a required standard, the hallmark of quality. An *M* surmounted with a crown meant that the piece was made in Mexico City. With Mexican independence in 1821, the crown above the *M* was replaced with a small *o*.

BUCARELI MONSTRANCE

Anonymous, mid 1700s, silver and gold, 69.67 troy weight, 23 3/4"h; 9 1/2" diameter of base (right)

A monstrance, also called an ostensorium, is a vessel in which the Eucharistic Host is carried in procession or exposed at the altar during certain devotional ceremonies. The Latin word *monstrare* translates "to show." Popular devotion to the Eucharistic Host developed in the fourteenth century. Monstrances were first used in France and Germany.

Fashioned of pure silver and covered by gold, this important piece has elaborate repoussé decoration on the scalloped base and stem. The base is inscribed in Spanish, and the dedication is described below. Hallmarks signifying Mexico's chief assayer, the taxation and quality of the metal are also inscribed. The head of the monstrance has 48 incised sunburst rays and is decorated with applied cherub heads. In the center of the sunburst is the gold and glass luna which holds the Host.

The Bucareli Monstrance has an interesting history. Father Serra requisitioned a monstrance for Mission San Francisco de Assisi, also known as Mission Dolores, in San Francisco.

After the monstrance arrived in Monterey and was brought to Carmel, Father Serra wrote to Bucareli in July, 1778. He wrote of the excitement upon opening the gift: "…I at once had them open, before any other, the case which contained so precious a prize …Just the very sight of the neat packing box or casing in which it came— which alone indicated that it was much bigger than the one we have here in the Mission—was cause enough for much jubilant anticipation. But how much greater was our joy when we took off the coverings and looked and looked at it with wondering eyes. Everyone was highly delighted with it. We gave a thousand thanks to God, and for your Excellency's kindness we begged a thousand blessings."

Finding the engraved inscription upon the base, Serra was genuinely surprised! In Spanish, it read:

> "Belonging to Carmel in New California donated by the Most Excellent Lord Knight Commander Sir Antonio Bucareli y Ursua, Viceroy of New Spain, and in the year of 1777."

Seeing this inscription, Serra fittingly chose to retain the gift from the Viceroy and send Mission Carmel's monstrance, which had been acquired from Mexico's Loreto Mission, to San Francisco.

SILVER CHALICE

Unknown, Mexico, 1791–1805, silver, gold, 22 ounces troy weight
9 ¹/₂"h; 5 ³/₄"d; 3 ¹/₄" cup diameter

In the Gospels of Matthew, Mark, Luke and John, as well as the Letter to the Corinthians I, the writings all include accounts of the Jesus' institution of the Eucharist. In the fourth century, the Roman Empire recognized Christianity, and gold and silver materials appeared in the creation of cups or chalices used during Mass as Eucharistic vessels.

This chalice of gilt silver is of extremely fine workmanship and has an intricate design. The base is scalloped, and the cup has elaborate repoussé and chased design. As was the custom, it has several hallmarks to note its composition and date of work. The upside-down crowned M between Pillars of Hercules indicate that the legal standard of silver was used and that taxes were paid. The eagle on cactus signifies the purity of the metal. An additional decree, promulgated in 1733, required that each silver piece bear the mark of the current chief assessor. The FCDA mark of Mexico's chief assayer is that of Antonio Forcada y la Plaza, whose term was from 1792–1818.

Often thought to be the chalice that Father Serra used, this seems not so. The Carmel Mission Informe of 1805 lists the chalice as a new addition to the Mission. Therefore, this chalice must have been created 1792–1805, whereas Father Serra had died in 1784.

It is in excellent condition. In modern times it was used by Pope John Paul II during his visit to Carmel Mission and the Monterey Diocese in 1985.

Unkown, Mexico, circa mid 17th century, silver, 12" x 10"

These altar pieces, known as the *Lavabo* and the *Palabrero*, were used during Mass from the sixteenth to twentieth centuries. A set of three prayer cards was placed on the altar. These two remain from mission days. The Mexican silver cards have chased lettering of Latin prayers, bordered with a repoussé design and mounted on wood.

A symbol of spiritual and physical cleansing, the *Lavabo* rite is performed by the priest when he washes his fingers before consecrating the host. The Latin word *lavabo* is taken from Psalm 26:6-12, "I will wash my hands …." Today, the priest says, "Lord, wash away my iniquity; cleanse me from my sin."

The *Palabrero* altar card is inscribed with the Latin, "*Initium Sancta Evangelii secondum Joannem* …." This refers to the beginning of the

Gospel of John. It was recited by the priest as he cleaned the chalice at the conclusion of the Mass. It was removed from mass prayers during the 1960s, after Vatican Council II.

The third altar card is not in the Mission collection. It would have the chased letters of the "*Munda Cor Meum*" prayer, words spoken before the Gospel proclamation. In modern times, the priest bows before the altar and quietly says, "Almighty God, cleanse my heart and my lips that I may worthily proclaim your Gospel," before he reads aloud the daily scripture passage.

Today all mass prayers are in a book called the "Pontifical Canon" and are usually spoken in the vernacular.

These altar cards came from Mission Loreto in Baja, California.

LAvabo inter innocentes manus meas: & circumdabo altare tuum Domine.

Ut audiam vocem laudis: & enarrem universa mirabilia tua.

Domine dilexi decorem domus tuæ: & locum habitationis gloriæ tuæ.

Ne perdas impiis animam meam: & cum viris sanguinum vitam meam.

In quorum manibus iniquitates sunt: dextera eorum repleta st muneribus.

Ego autem in innocentia mea ingressus sum: redime me & miserere mei.

Pes meus stetit in directo: in Ecclesiis benedicam te Domine.

Gloria Patri, & Filio, & Spiritui sancto. Sicut erat, &c.

Ultimæ Collectæ addendum

Et famulos tuos Papam, N. Antistitem nostrum, N. Regem nostrum, cum prole regia, cum populo & exercitu sibi commissis, ab omni adversitate custodi: pacem tuam nostris concede temporibus & ab Ecclesia tua cunctam repelle nequitiam. Per Dominum.

SILVER ASPERGES BUCKET

Anonymous, Mexico, second half of the 17th century, silver, 17" x 11¼"

This bucket holds water, blessed by the priest, and is used to bless the congregation, the altar or the coffin of a deceased person. The Asperges Rite is a symbol of spiritual cleansing. Its name is derived from the Latin words that begin the rite, *Asperges me, Domine hyssopo, et mundobor*, which translates, "Lord, sprinkle me with hyssop, and I shall be cleansed," from Psalm 51:7. The rite has been in use from at least the tenth century, and it is most often used at the beginning of a Mass.

The bucket of hammered silver has hand-engraved scenes and figures on the central section. One engraving is of Saint Ignatius Loyola, founder of the Jesuits, with a book and three nails representing the crucifixion of Jesus. The etched *IHS* monogram is an often-used Jesuit symbol, the first three Greek letters in the name Jesus, later Latinized to *Jesu Hominum Salvatori*. Also on the bucket is an engraving of the Christ Child holding a globe. Another engraved scene is the Annunciation, recalling the Angel Gabriel's announcement to Mary that she would be the mother of the Savior.

Below the central section are a raised pedestal and a bulbous section. A repoussé decoration encircles both sections. Above the central section, the bucket widens with a scalloped design. Lion heads decorate the bases of the arabesque-designed hollow handle.

Its Mexican origin is attested by the silver hallmarks on the inside rim. This piece was probably among the silver furnishings that Father Serra brought with him to Alta California in 1769 as it does not appear in any of the original requisitional documents. It is the oldest documented piece in the silver collection. The Jesuit iconography links it to a Jesuit mission, no doubt in Baja California from which Serra brought it north.

There probably was a matching aspergillium, the sprinkler which is dipped into the water to bless those nearby, but the original is not in the Mission collection.

DIVINE SHERPHERDESS

Anonymous, Mexico, circa 1800, oil on canvas, 72" x 48"

The Divine Shepherdess is a painting that commemorates the apparition of the Virgin Mary, dressed as a shepherdess, to a Franciscan named Isidore of Seville (1662–1750) in the year 1703. In this painting, Mary is reminiscent of the image of Christ as the Good Shepherd. There are many paintings of the *Divine Shepherdess* and devotion to her in this capacity spread rapidly through Spain and the New World where she was venerated by missionaries and converts alike.

The Carmel Mission painting is one of two rolled paintings in the Mission collection. Rolled paintings were often of favorite images or saints and were frequently used in mission work. They were composed on a thin canvas with a wooden box attached enabling them to be rolled up and easily transported from mission to mission. In the remote, agrarian outposts of mission work, these paintings could be used in makeshift settings for devotion or services, and the container protected them from damage during travel.

Isidore of Seville claimed that the Virgin told him that if he would honor her under this guise, as a shepherdess, she would assist him with his apostolic labors. So moved by this event, he is said to have commissioned a painting of the vision. He described the details to the artist as follows: The Virgin should be at the center of the composition, seated on a rock under a tree. She is to be clothed in a red gown, a blue mantle and a shepherdess's hat. A shepherd's crook is close at hand. She is feeding roses to a flock of sheep gathered around her. In the distance, a lone sheep, pursued by a wolf, is uttering the words "*Ave Maria.*" St. Michael is coming to the lost sheep's rescue. The background scene with the wolf, sheep and St. Michael recalls the parable of the lost sheep in Luke's Gospel.

Although Isidore's vision became the standard iconography for the image of *The Divine Shepherdess*, variations in iconographic detail were not unusual. In the Mission's painting, the Christ Child is seated on the Virgin's lap and is the one who holds the shepherd's crook and feeds roses to the sheep. The eyes of the sheep have a human quality underscoring the symbolism of sheep representing the human flock of Christianity. The Carmel painting also shows four angels, two of whom are holding a crown over the Virgin's head.

VIRGIN OF LIGHT

Anonymous, Mexico, late 1800s, oil on canvas, 40½" x 31½"

Devotion to the *Virgin of Light* originates from the city of Palermo, Sicily, as early as 1682. Versions of this subject matter replicate a miraculous painting from Sicily said to have been created in 1722. José María Genovese, S.J. brought a copy of the painting to New Spain in 1732. It was sent to León, Guanajuato, where it remains enshrined in the former Jesuit church, now the Cathedral. The cult of the Virgin of Light grew rapidly in Mexico during the eighteenth century. Originally the title of the work was *Mother of Light*, but popular usage in Mexico established its current title.

The painting at Carmel Mission is one of many copies done by various Mexican artists. There is some speculation that the Carmel painting may have been originally at Mission San Buenaventura then brought to Carmel Mission in the early 1800s after Mission San Buenaventura was damaged in an earthquake.

This painting follows the original painting's composition closely. It depicts the Virgin carrying the infant Jesus who is receiving flaming hearts from a basket offered by an angel. In her other hand, Mary grabs the hand of a young man who represents a soul in danger of being lost.

In the original painting the young man appeared to be pulled out of the mouth of hell. In the late eighteenth century, this aspect of the painting's iconography became controversial. The Church did not want it to appear that one could receive salvation directly from the Virgin. It was resolved that in future representations the Virgin would be holding the soul up, protecting one from falling, not pulling one out of hell. Therefore, in the Carmel Mission painting, the young man is being dangled in front of the flames, thus avoiding the controvercy. Also of note in the Carmel painting and, not in the original, is the Franciscan in the lower right who is offering up a flaming heart.

The Virgin is dressed in a white gown with a blue mantle around her shoulders and held aloft on a cloud of cherubim. Two angels hold a crown over her head, which reinforces her status as Queen of Heaven.

This Carmel Mission painting is a rolled canvas with a wooden carrying case attached to the thin canvas, making it portable for travel to and from various missions or ranches for services or fiestas.

LA MADRE SANTISSIMA DE LA LUZ.

FOUNDING PAINTING

Léon Trousset, California, USA, 1877, oil on canvas, 53" x 72"

The Founding Painting is a work of oil on canvas, painted by artist Léon Trousset (1838–1917). Trousset was born and raised in France, but little is known about him, his training or his paintings prior to his time in Mexico and the western United States. Trousset became known in California as a painter of landscapes, architectural and historical scenes, and city views of the type then popular in lithographs. He lived in Texas and Arizona in the 1860s and in Mazatlán in 1874. By 1875, he was painting in northern California and Monterey where, for a short time, he was an important personality in the fledgling art colony.

Trousset arrived in Monterey in the fall of 1875 and painted a watercolor entitled *The City of Monterey, November first, 1875*. In 1876, Trousset visited southern California where he worked briefly. He produced two large religious scenes entitled *Resurrection of Christ* and *The Assumption of the Blessed Virgin Mary* for the Church of St. Vibiana in Los Angeles. He later returned to the Monterey area where he and a fellow French artist, Alexander Zins, were commissioned to make paintings for churches in Monterey and other California cities.

In 1876 and 1877, Trousset produced a number of paintings depicting the founding of the mission in Monterey and Father Serra's first Mass, which took place beneath a large oak tree on the Monterey shore on June 3, 1770. The location of the Mass in Monterey was thought to be the spot where, in 1602, Sebastian Vizcaíno's expedition celebrated the Eucharist. Because there is only one boat visible in the painting, whereas Vizcaíno came with three, it is clear that the celebrant was meant to be Serra himself. It was during the Vizcaíno expedition, however, that the Carmelites briefly explored the bays of Monterey, Carmel and the river. They chose the name *Carmelo* for the area and river, making these place names some of the oldest in America.

The focus of the painting is the makeshift altar consisting of an oak tree with a large white cloth canopy attached to the branches. Father Serra is shown with hands uplifted raising the host. Six large candlesticks on the altar, possibly those used by Serra during his life at Carmel Mission, and still on the altar today, are shown in the painting. Two other friars are celebrating Mass with him, thought to be the two who accompanied him on the de Portolà expedition, Father Juan Crespi and Father Francisco Palóu, who became Father Serra's biographer. The military personnel are shown in attendance and some natives are looking on.

The Carmel Mission painting is the largest of the paintings representing this event. It was donated to the Mission in 1922, but there is no record of the donor or where the painting was from 1877–1922. The painting was loaned to the Crocker Art Museum of Sacramento in 2007 for the traveling exhibition *Artists at Continent's End*.

Trousset left California soon after the painting was completed in 1877. By 1879 he was in Durango, Mexico, where he left behind a painting of that town. He traveled to other places in Mexico and was in Texas and New Mexico in 1885 and 1886 producing views and architectural scenes. He finally settled in Juarez, Mexico, where he married María Jesús Bustos. They adopted a son, Antonio. Trousset died in Mexico on December 29, 1917.

WAKING OF THE APOSTLES IN GETHSEMANE

E. Carlton Fortune, Monterey, California, USA, 1942, oil on canvas, 72" x 48"

The Waking of the Apostles in Gethsemane is displayed only during the Lenten season. This painting depicts Jesus Christ in the Garden of Gethsemane. Following the Jewish Passover dinner, Jesus asked his disciples to retire with him to the Mount of Olives to pray. He went into the garden with three of his disciples, Peter, James and John, leaving the others at the edge of the grove. This was just hours before Jesus was turned over to the officials to be crucified. He was suffering emotional agony, knowing that Judas would betray him, and the nature of his death. He asked the three disciples to stay awake with him and pray. However, when he returned from where he went to pray privately, the disciples were asleep, and he was greatly disappointed.

In this painting, Jesus stands in the center wearing a white robe with a green sash over his left shoulder. His hand is turned up as a signal to the apostles to awake. Two men sit on the ground on the right side of the painting with their heads slumped as if sleeping. A third figure is behind them looking into the painting. There is a large rock behind Christ, perhaps as an iconic reference to Jesus building his church on the rock of Peter. The city of Jerusalem appears in the background.

This work was painted in 1942 by E. (Euphemia) Charlton Fortune. She painted it for the Cathedral of Kansas City. Later it was moved to their archdiocesan seminary where it was eventually purchased by Monsignor Robert B. Brennan and given to Carmel Mission.

E. Charlton Fortune was born in 1885 in Sausalito, Marin County, California. She studied at Mark Hopkins Institute and Saint John Wood School of Art in London. Unfortunately, all of Fortune's earliest works were destroyed in the 1906 San Francisco earthquake and fire. She then began working in New York, illustrating for Harpers Magazine. In 1910, having moved back to San Francisco, she obtained a position with Sunset Magazine.

This painting exemplifies the second phase of Fortune's art career. She initially gained recognition for her landscapes that were done in the style of the post-impressionist period and became one of the most eminent California artists in this genre during the 1920s and 1930s. In 1913, she and her mother began to vacation in Carmel, and Effie (her nick-name) chose Monterey for her permanent home in 1927. There she joined the Carmel Art Association which remains active today.

In 1934–35, she founded the Monterey Guild of Religious Art, producing much religious art for various Catholic institutions. She crisscrossed the United States obtaining and working on commissions for paintings, sculptures, vestments and designs of church interiors. She remained focused on religious art during her remaining years. She died in 1969 in Monterey. Her work is in the permanent collections of the California Palace of Legion of Honor, San Francisco Fine Art Museum and the Monterey Museum of Art in Monterey, California.

Andrews, Linda. *Conservator Report*, 2008. CA: Carmel Mission Docent Archives.

Attwater, Donald. *A Catholic Dictionary*. Rockford, IL: Tom Books and Publisher, Inc., 1997.

Ayme, E. "St. Rose of Lima." *Catholic Encyclopedia.* New York: Robert Appleton Company, 1912.

Baer, Kurt. *Notes from the Kurt Baer Collection.* Santa Barbara, CA: California Mission Archives.

Bargellini, Clara. Spanish-Colonial art historian, Universidad Nacional Autónoma de Mexico. On campus visit, 2007.

Bargellini, Clara and Michael K. Komanecky. *The Arts of the Missions of Northern New Spain 1600–1821.* Mexico: Antiguo Colegio de San Ildefonso, Mexico City, 2009.

Borrell, M. *The Grandeur Of Viceregal Mexico - Treasures From The Museo.* Houston, TX: The Museum of Fine Arts, 2002.

Boylan, Leona Davis. *Spanish Colonial Silver.* NM: Museum of New Mexico Press in cooperation with The International Folk Art Foundation, 1994.

Brunelle, Mark. *Fray Junipero Serra.* Carmel-by-the-Sea, CA: Dobronte Publications, 1987.

Burke, Marcus B. *Treasures of Mexican Colonial Painting.* Davenport, IA: Davenport Museum of Art, 1998.

Carmel Docent Archive Files. Report from Hoover Presidential Library and Museum, West Branch, Iowa. 2007.

Chase, John and Charles Saunders. *The California Padres and their Missions.* Whitefish, MT: Kessinger Publishing, 1915.

DeNevi, Don and Noel Francis Moholy. *Junipero Serra.* New York: Harper & Row Publishers, 1985.

Downie, Harry. *Audio Tapes.* Courtesy of Miriam Downie, daughter of Mr. Downie.

Ellsberg, Robert. *All Saints, Daily Reflections on Saints, Prophets, and Witnesses for Our Time.* New York: The Crossroads Publishing Company, 2004.

Engelhardt, Fr. Zephyrin O.F.M. *Mission San Carlos Borromeo.* Ramona, CA: Ballena Press, 1973.

Encyclopedia of Latin American and Caribbean Art. New York: Macmillan Publishers, 2000.

Encyclopedia of the Nations, Volume 3, Americas/ Equador. New York: The World of Mark, 6th ed., 1984.

"Echos of Monterey's Past." *Game and Gossip Magazine.* Monterey, CA: What's Doing Publication, March 15, 1961.

Furguson, George. *Signs and Symbols in Christian Art.* New York: Oxford University Press, 1954.

Frank, Larry. *New Kingdom of the Saints: Religious Art of New Mexico 1780–1907.* NM: University of New Mexico Press, 1992.

Giorgi, Rosa. *Saints in Art.* Los Angeles, CA: Getty Trust Publications, J. Paul Getty Museum, 2003.

Hall, James. *Dictionary of Subjects and Symbols In Art.* New York: Harper and Row, 1974.

Hauk, Steve, Penny Perlmutter and Tina Flaherty. *E. Charlton Fortune: A Biography.* Carmel-by-the-Sea, CA: Carmel Art Association, 2001.

Hiller, Peter. "The Story of the Father Junipero Serra Memorial Cenotaph." Carmel Mission Basilica, 2006.

Hoover Institute Archives. Box 255. Press clippings-South American Trip.

Huckins, Pamela J., Ph.D. Candidate in Art History, New York University. Conversation, 2007.

Hughes, Edan M. *Artists In California, 1786–1940.* Ann Arbor, MI: Braun-Brumfeld Inc., 1986.

"Jo Mora, Artist and Writer." *Monterey Museum of Art Catalog.* Monterey, CA: 1998.

Kerr, Susan Anderson. "Preliminary Observations on Angels in Religious Art in New Spain." *Bolétin, The Journal of the California Mission Studies Association.* Volume 25, no. 2. 2008.

Mayer-Thurman, Christa C. *Raiment for the Lord's Service: A Thousand Years of Western Vestments.* Chicago, IL.: The Art Institute of Chicago, 1975.

Mendez, Ruben G. "Sacrament of the Sun: Eschatological Architecture and Solar Geometry in a California Mission." *Bolétin, The Journal of the California Mission Studies Association.* Volume 22, no. 1. 2005.

Menn, Richard. "2005 Condition Report." Archives of the Carmel Mission.

Morgado, Martin J. *Junípero Serra's Legacy.* Pacific Grove, CA: Mt. Carmel Publishing, 1987.

Murray, Peter and Linda Murray. *The Art of the Renaissance.* New York: Thames and Hudson Inc., 1985.

New American Bible. Sponsored by The Bishops' Committee of the Confraternity of Christian Doctrine. Iowa Falls, IA: World Bible Publishers, 1976.

Neuerburg, Norman. "La Madre Santisima de la Luz." *The Journal of San Diego History.* Spring 1995, Volume 41, no. 2.

Painting and Sculpture at Mission Santa Barbara. CA: Academy of American Franciscan History, 1953.

Pagliarulo, Sister Celeste. *Harry Downie and the Restoration of the Mission San Carlos Borromeo, 1931–1931.* CA: Historical Society of Southern California, 2004.

Perouse, Jean Francois de la. *Life In A California Mission: The Journals of Jean Francois de la Perouse.* Berkeley, CA: Heyday Books, reprinted 1989.

Pierce, Donna, Clara Bargellini and Rogelio Ruiz Gomar. *Painting A New World-Mexican Art and Life, 1521–1821.* CO: Denver Art Museum Catalog, 2004.

Ratzinger, Joseph, Pope Benedict XVI. *Jesus of Nazareth.* New York: Rizzoli International Publications, Inc., 2009.

Rowland, Leon. *Old Santa Cruz Mission.* 1941.

Shields, Scott A. *Artists at Continent's End: The Monterey Peninsula Art Colony 1875–1907.* Berkeley, CA: Crocker Art Museum, University of California Press, 2006.

Smith, Frances R. *The Architectural History of Mission San Carlos Borromeo.* CA: California Historical Survey Commission, 1921.

"St. Joseph in California Mission Art." *St. Joseph Magazine.* CA: Franciscan Fathers, Province of Santa Barbara, March, 1956.

Temple, Sidney. *The Carmel Mission.* Santa Cruz, CA: Western Tanager Press, 1980.

The Catholic Study Bible, New American Bible. New York/Oxford: Oxford University Press, 1989/1990.

The New American Bible. Wichita, KS: St. Jerome Press, 1987.

Tooney, Donald Francis. *The Spirit of California, Spanish Colonial Missions.* Santa Fe, NM: University of New Mexico Press, 2001.

Weber, Francis J. *The Life and Times of Junípero Serra.* San Luis Obispo, CA: EZ Nature Books, 1988.

Willinger, A.J., Bishop of Monterey. "Our Lady of Bethlehem" Pamphlet. CA: 1954.

Worship II, A Hymnal for Roman Catholic Parishes. Chicago, IL: G.I.A. Publications, Inc., 1975.

Zarur, Elizabeth N.C. and Charles Muir Lovell. *Art and Faith in Mexico-The Nineteenth Century Retablo Tradition.* Albuquerque, NM: University of New Mexico Press, 2001.